ChatGPT Simplified Unleash Creativity and Save Time in Your Daily Life (2024 Edition)

ChatGPT Simplified Unleash Creativity and Save Time in Your Daily Life (2024 Edition)

LEARN HOW TO EXTRACT THE MOST VALUE OUT OF AI.

Nick Ruffilo

Zen of Technology Press

Contents

1

Introduction

Welcome to the world of Artificial Intelligence (AI) – a realm where the future is unfolding right before our eyes. You've probably heard the buzz about ChatGPT; it's been making headlines and captivating over 110 million users worldwide. But if you're among those who haven't explored it yet, you're in for a delightful discovery. In this guide, I'm excited to unveil how even the free version of ChatGPT can revolutionize your daily life, sparking your creativity, saving precious time, and enhancing your everyday experiences.

I don't believe this is just hyperbole. This new breed of AI will be as ubiquitous soon as the internet is today. On a daily basis, we check our email, the weather, social networks, and play games. Taking an entire day away from the internet is actually a difficult task, and besides when immersing ourselves in nature, is often a less satisfying one. Using weather apps to plan your day, sharing laughs and building connections through social media, and getting important information via email - all of these things improve our daily life.

AI will become crucially important, and learning to use it now will only improve that future relationship. Imagine having a copy of yourself to bounce ideas off of - and better yet, that copy has access to the entire world's knowledge. From party planning, helping you write a difficult email to a coworker, or developing a meal plan - AI can be a powerful tool.

Think AI is just a futuristic concept? Think again. For the past decade, AI has been your silent partner in everyday life. It's the voice of Alexa as it dims your smart home lights, the helpful hints from Siri on your iPhone, and the convenience of Google's AI assistant as it navigates your day. Ever interacted with an automated help line? That's AI in action, albeit in its more basic form. Now, imagine something far more advanced yet astonishingly user-friendly. That's ChatGPT – a powerhouse tool that combines the simplicity of these services with cutting-edge technology to deliver immediate, tangible benefits to your life. Ready to dive in?

In the pages that follow, we'll embark on a fascinating journey through a variety of everyday scenarios where ChatGPT can be your ultimate ally. From crafting the perfect meal plan to organizing a memorable birthday bash, from navigating the complexities of job hunting to selecting the ideal gift, this guide has you covered. But that's not all – I'll also unveil the secrets to unlocking your creative potential with the help of AI. And, to ensure you're fully equipped, I'll guide you through the art of crafting effective prompts, empowering you to extract the most insightful and helpful responses from ChatGPT. So, whether you're a tech newbie or just looking for fresh ways to streamline your life, you're in the right place!

Before we dive in, it's crucial to understand both the strengths and the limitations of ChatGPT. At its core, ChatGPT is an LLM – a Large Language Model. This impressive technology has been trained on vast amounts of text, learning to associate words, concepts, and the nuances of grammar. Thanks to this extensive training, ChatGPT can offer insights or guidance on an incredibly wide range of topics.

However, it's important to note a significant caveat: ChatGPT is not an infallible source of truth or facts. For instance, if you ask 'When is US Independence Day celebrated?', ChatGPT would correctly say 'July 4th', but this response is based on the high frequency of this association in its training data, not on an intrinsic understanding of historical events. Be aware that ChatGPT might occasionally provide inaccurate information, particularly on sensitive or controversial subjects. It's essential to approach its responses with a critical eye and verify the information independently.

That said, despite these limitations, ChatGPT has been an extraordinarily helpful companion in my life for over six months. In this guide, I'm excited to share with you the valuable lessons I've learned and how to make the most of this groundbreaking tool.

2

Getting Started

Embarking on your ChatGPT journey begins with setting up an account. And here's the good news: you have options to suit your needs and budget. For beginners or those just exploring, the free version of ChatGPT offers a solid foundation. It grants you basic access, perfectly adequate for getting a feel of what this AI can do. But if you're looking for more advanced capabilities, consider the paid version. Priced at $20 per month, it unlocks a suite of enhanced features, which I'll delve into in relevant sections of this guide.

In this guide, I'll mainly be showcasing examples from ChatGPT version 4.0. While this version is currently available for limited use, the free version operates on ChatGPT version 3.5. It's true that you might notice a difference in the quality of results between these versions, but don't let that deter you. The world of AI technology evolves rapidly, and it's likely that the more advanced capabilities of version 4.0 will become accessible in the free version before you know it.

To create an account go to https://chat.openai.com/. There are ChapGPT apps on iOS and Android, but you can use the website just fine from your mobile device, laptop, or desktop. You can sign up using your Google account, Microsoft account, Apple account, or create a new account with your email address.

With your ChatGPT account ready to go, you're now at the

threshold of a world where AI meets everyday life. Prepare to embark on a journey of discovery, innovation, and enhanced productivity. Let's dive in and unlock the full potential of ChatGPT to transform your daily routines, boost your creativity, and streamline your tasks. The future of personalized AI assistance begins now!

Once you have your account and are signed in, you will see this screen:

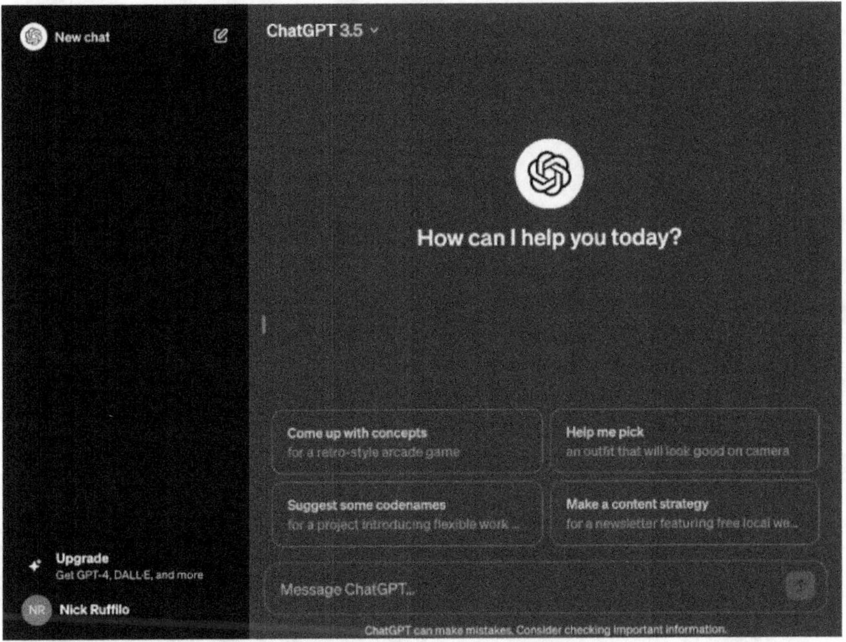

Start screen for ChatGPT

Up in the top left of your screen, you willl see a "New chat" button. This will start a new conversation with ChatGPT. ChatGPT will remember any previous chat in a conversation, so if you don't want to use previous prompts, start a new conversation for each topic. Previous chats will be visible below that button as you create them.

The free version of ChatGPT is version 3.5. To access the latest version, version 4.0, you will need to pay $20/mo for a membership.

If you are using your phone, you'll see the following:

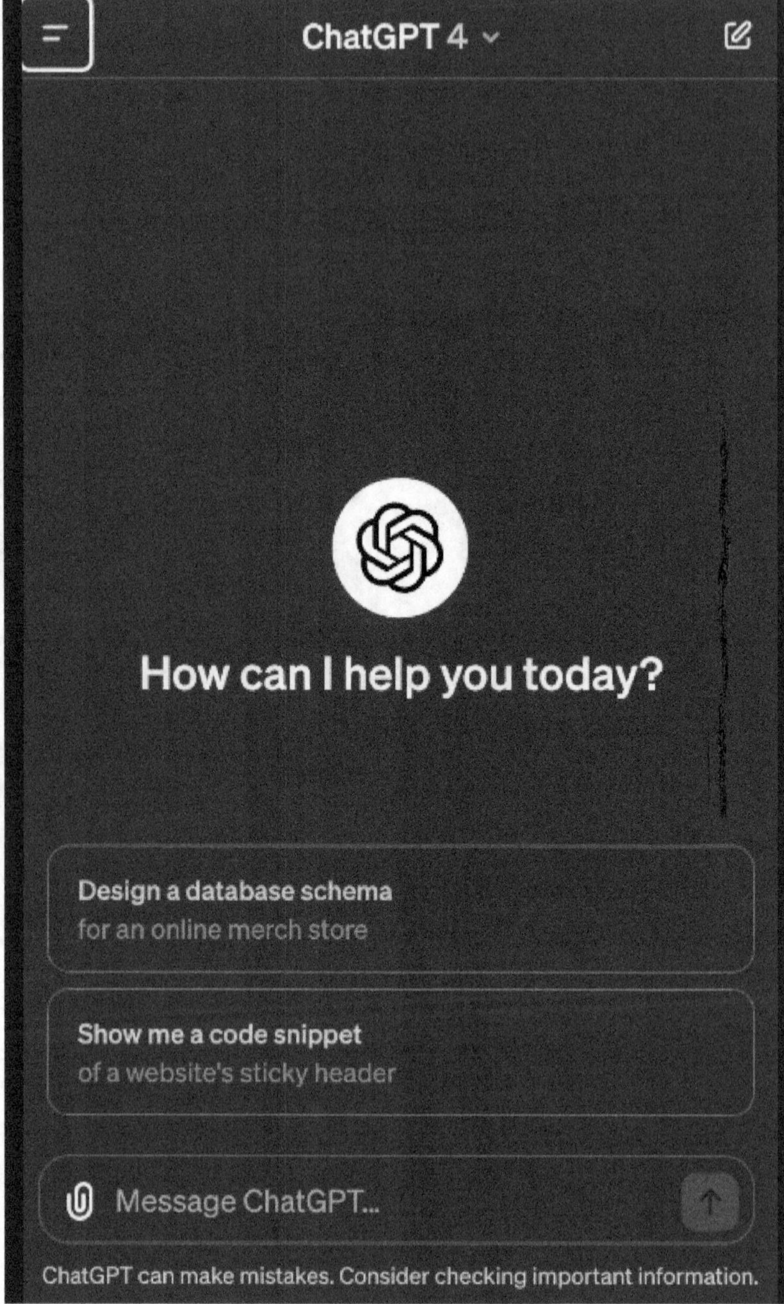

Mobile view of ChatGPT

If you wish to see your previous conversations, tap the two line in the top left of the screen. The rest of the instructions apply to both the mobile and desktop sites.

At the bottom of your screen you willl see the prompt "Message ChatGPT." This is where you will type in your message. Ultimately you can say or ask anything, but the questions you ask are called "prompts."

Now let's start having some fun!

3

Meal Planning

I have a son who is 12 years old and particular about the types of foods he will eat, and a wife who is gluten-free. While eating out is easy, as everyone can order exactly what they want, when it comes to cooking at home and lunch planning for school, it gets a bit more complicated. That is, until I started using ChatGPT!

The more information you provide ChatGPT, the better the results you will get. A simple prompt like: "Give me 10 meal options for a 12 year old" will be much more generic than, "Give me 10 meal options for a 12 year old that include items like peppers, onions, mac and cheese, pasta, and grilled cheese, but do not include mayonnaise, eggs, ham, or potatoes." Additionally, once you get your response, you can always revise. You can add things like "no soups" or "generate 10 more, but include salads." If you like the list, you can even ask for the ingredients as a shopping list. In a matter of minutes, you can have a weeks worth of lunches and dinners planned, and a grocery list!

You can also provide a list of ingredients that you have available and ask for meals that can be made. Now, as noted before, ChatGPT does not know truth or facts, so it is always possible that it will give you recommendations that utilize items not listed. If that is the case, you can tell it to refine the options with whatever item you would like removed.

Lets take a look at what some of these prompts / interactions look like in the wild:

Me: Give me 10 meal options for a 12 year old that include items like peppers, onions, mac and cheese, pasta, and grilled cheese, but do not include mayonnaise, eggs, ham, or potatoes.

ChatGPT

Certainly! Here are ten meal options for a 12-year-old that include ingredients like peppers, onions, mac and cheese, pasta, and grilled cheese, while avoiding mayonnaise, eggs, ham, and potatoes:

Veggie Pasta: Whole wheat pasta tossed with sautéed bell peppers, onions, and a tomato-based sauce. You can add some grated cheese on top for extra flavor.

Grilled Cheese with a Twist: A classic grilled cheese sandwich with added sliced bell peppers and onions for a crunchy, flavorful twist.

Mac and Cheese with Veggies: Prepare traditional mac and cheese and stir in some sautéed bell peppers and onions for added nutrition and taste.

Stuffed Bell Peppers: Bell peppers stuffed with a mixture of cooked rice, onions, a bit of cheese, and Italian seasoning, then baked until tender.

Vegetable Stir-Fry with Noodles: A colorful stir-fry with bell peppers, onions, and other veggies, served over noodles with a light soy sauce or teriyaki sauce.

Cheesy Onion Flatbread: A simple flatbread topped with caramelized onions, bell peppers, and a generous amount of melted cheese, baked until golden.

Pasta Primavera: A pasta dish with a variety of vegetables like bell peppers and onions, tossed in olive oil and garlic, and sprinkled with Parmesan cheese.

Vegetable Quesadilla: A quesadilla filled with sautéed onions, bell peppers, and cheese, cooked until the tortilla is crispy and the cheese is melted.

Veggie Pizza: Homemade or store-bought pizza dough topped with tomato sauce, bell peppers, onions, and cheese, then baked until the crust is crispy and the cheese is bubbly.

Vegetable Fajitas: Sautéed bell peppers and onions served with warm tortillas, cheese, and a variety of toppings like salsa or sour cream (optional).

These meals are versatile, allowing for variations according to personal taste preferences and dietary needs. They are also simple enough for a 12-year-old to enjoy and can be nutritious and satisfying.

* * *

Me: For the items listed, can you give me a list of ingredients so that I can buy them in a grocery store

ChatGPT

Certainly! Here's a shopping list covering the ingredients for the meal options I mentioned:

Fresh Produce

Bell peppers (various colors)
Onions (yellow or red)
Garlic
Optional additional vegetables for stir-fry, fajitas, and pasta primavera (like carrots, broccoli, snap peas)

Dairy

Cheddar cheese (for mac and cheese, grilled cheese, quesadillas)
Parmesan cheese (for pasta dishes)
Mozzarella cheese (for pizza)
Butter (for cooking and grilled cheese)
Milk (for mac and cheese)

Pasta & Grains

Whole wheat pasta (for veggie pasta, pasta primavera)
Macaroni (for mac and cheese)
Rice (for stuffed bell peppers)
Noodles (for stir-fry)
Tortillas (for quesadillas, fajitas)
Flatbread or pizza dough (for onion flatbread, veggie pizza)

Canned & Jarred Goods

Tomato sauce (for pasta dishes, pizza)
Canned or jarred salsa (for fajitas, quesadillas)
Soy sauce or teriyaki sauce (for stir-fry)

Baking & Spices

Italian seasoning (for stuffed peppers, pasta dishes)
Olive oil (for cooking and pasta dishes)
Salt & pepper

Optional Extras

Sour cream (for fajitas, quesadillas)
Your favorite stir-fry veggies or pizza toppings

This list includes basic ingredients for the meals. You can adjust quantities based on the number of servings you need and your personal preferences. Don't forget to check your pantry for some of these items before shopping to avoid duplicates!

If you want specific cooking instructions and an exact recipe that you are looking to follow, I recommend instead using Google and finding a recipe on a website or a blog, as I would not trust cooking times or instructions from ChatGPT. But immediately, you have a list of options that include your favorite items and exclude items that you want to avoid. If you would like more options, all you have to do is ask "list 10 more items" and it will do so.

4

Birthday Party / Event Planning

We've all been in a situation where we know we want to have a party, but we aren't quite sure what to do. What are some party theme ideas? What are some party games we can play? What are some ideas for goodie bags? Whether it is a birthday party, a charity event, a graduation party, or any other reason to celebrate, ChatGPT can help!

Start by sharing as much information about the party as you can. Who is hosting the party, what is your budget, and what is known about the subject of the event. Also be clear about what you are looking for. Below is the response for the following prompt: "I am turning 40 and I want to have a birthday celebration. I like playing board games, party games, and making things. I am not a big alcohol drinker. I would like it to be somewhat small, less than 30 people and will have access to spaces that will accommodate that many people. Please suggest 3 party ideas, unique party invites for each idea, and a few themed foods that I can serve."

Happy early 40th birthday! It's great that you have specific interests and a clear idea of the size and scope of your celebration.

Here are three party ideas tailored to your preferences, along with unique invitation suggestions and themed food ideas for each:

1. Board Game Bash

Party Theme: A cozy, fun-filled evening where guests can dive into various board games. You can have different tables set up for different types of games — strategy, trivia, and classic board games.

Invitation Idea: Design invitations to look like popular board game boxes or cards, with details on the back. For instance, a Monopoly-style card with "Advance to [Your Name]'s 40th Birthday Bash".

Themed Foods:

Dice Cheese Cubes: Small cubes of different cheeses arranged to look like dice.

Checkerboard Sandwiches: Sandwiches cut and arranged in a checkerboard pattern, with different fillings to create contrast.

Game Piece Cookies: Cookies decorated to look like various board game pieces (e.g., chess pieces, Monopoly tokens).

2. Creative Craft Party

Party Theme: A hands-on party where guests can engage in different crafting activities, like painting, pottery, or DIY projects. This can be both fun and a great way for everyone to take home a personalized souvenir.

Invitation Idea: Send out crafty, handmade invitations with a small DIY element for the recipient to complete, like a simple origami fold or a color-in section.

Themed Foods:

Palette Platters: Serve snacks on painter's palettes (clean and food-safe) with an array of colorful dips.

Edible Craft Tools: Cookies or pastries shaped like craft tools (scissors, paintbrushes, etc.).

Fruit Sculptures: Create fruit arrangements that mimic popular art sculptures or abstract art pieces.

3. Party Game Gala

Party Theme: A night filled with laughter and energy, featuring a variety of party games like charades, Pictionary, or even interactive video games that get everyone moving.

Invitation Idea: Design the invitation to look like a game show flyer, with bright colors and fun fonts. Add a 'ticket' to the Game Gala as part of the invite.

Themed Foods:

Puzzle Piece Sandwiches: Cut sandwiches into interlocking puzzle pieces.

Game Controller Cake Pops: Cake pops decorated to look like various game controllers.

Character Cupcakes: Cupcakes decorated to resemble icons from famous party games.

For each of these themes, you can further enhance the atmosphere with appropriate decorations and music. Enjoy planning your birthday celebration!

Whether you are throwing a 40th birthday bash, pickleball fundraiser, or a kids birthday party, you can see how this can greatly speed up idea creation and planning. You can then dive deeper and ask it to get you decoration ideas, and again, even a shopping list.

5

Job Search Advice / Self Improvement

ChatGPT is no replacement for a therapist or a life coach, but when it comes to smaller pieces of advice, it's ease and quickness are unmatched. I will touch specifically upon job search help, then general self improvement.

Resume Improvement

I struggle when it comes to writing good descriptions of what I did at a company. How do you sum up years of work in a few sentences? How do you clearly explain roles and responsibilities? This is something that ChatGPT does with ease. Explain what you do in your job, with as much detail as possible then ask ChatGPT to summarize it for use in a resume.

An advanced tactic when it comes to prompts in ChatGPT is to give ChatGPT more context into its frame of reference. Before your prompt, try adding: "You are a resume bot. Your goal is to create descriptions of jobs that would clearly explain the roles and responsibilities at a job and make hiring managers want to hire the candidate."

Sure, it's long, but it will allow ChatGPT to pull more associations from the job search and resume-building content that it has processed.

Great, you now have clean job descriptions, what next? Describe what you are looking for, what you have access to, and that you need a plan of action. Here's a sample prompt and it's output:

"I have been working as a barista for 5 years and managed a Starbucks for 5 years. I am looking for retail management positions. I would like to get out of food services and ideally work for a clothing outlet. What are some skills I might need and what is a plan of action for finding and applying to these jobs."

ChatGPT:

Transitioning from a food service management position to a retail management role, especially in a clothing outlet, can be a strategic move. Your experience as a barista and manager at Starbucks has likely equipped you with many transferable skills. Here's a breakdown of the skills you might need and a plan of action for finding and applying to these jobs:

Skills Needed

Customer Service Excellence: You already have this from your barista experience. Retail, like food service, demands a high level of customer interaction and satisfaction.

Inventory Management: Understanding stock levels, ordering, and inventory rotation will be crucial.

Visual Merchandising: This is more specific to retail, particularly clothing outlets. The ability to display products in an appealing way is key.

Sales and Marketing: While you may have some experience from Starbucks, retail clothing may require a different approach to sales techniques and promotions.

Staff Management and Training: Your experience here will be directly transferable. However, you'll need to adapt to the specifics of retail staffing.

Financial Management: Skills in managing budgets, reducing costs, and increasing profitability are highly valuable.

Tech Savvy: Familiarity with retail-specific software and point-of-sale systems could be beneficial.

Plan of Action

Upgrade Your Skills: If there are gaps in your skills (like visual merchandising), consider taking short courses or certifications. Online platforms like Coursera or LinkedIn Learning offer relevant courses.

Update Your Resume: Highlight your transferable skills. Emphasize your management experience, customer service skills, and any sales-related achievements.

Network: Use LinkedIn to connect with people in the retail industry. Attend local networking events or retail industry conferences.

Research Companies: Identify clothing outlets you're interested in. Learn about their company culture, values, and what they look for in their employees.

Tailor Your Applications: When applying, tailor your application to each specific company. Show how your past experience is relevant to managing a retail store.

Prepare for Interviews: Be ready to discuss how your experience in food service management will benefit you in a retail environment. Have specific examples ready.

Consider Entry-Level Positions: If necessary, be open to starting in a slightly lower position to gain specific industry experience.

Utilize Job Search Platforms: Websites like Indeed, Glassdoor, or LinkedIn can be great resources for finding job openings in retail management.

Seek Feedback: After interviews, ask for feedback to improve your approach in future applications.

Stay Informed: Keep up-to-date with retail trends, especially in fashion and clothing. This will show potential employers that you are passionate and informed about the industry.

Remember, your experience in managing a Starbucks is a strong foundation. It demonstrates your ability to handle a fast-paced environment, manage a team, and maintain customer satisfaction, all of which are critical in retail management. Good luck!

Chat GPT can also role play. You can tell it to play a specific role, and it will do just that. When it comes to job search, you can continue your conversation using the prompt: "Pretend that you are the hiring manager for the role of Retail Manager. Ask me 5 interview questions then analyze my responses". Chat GPT will ask you 5 questions and you will be able to respond and it will give you feedback on your responses.

$$6$$

Gift Ideas

For me, finding the right gift is really hard. Or at least, it used to be. Sure, there are "gift guides for co-workers" but personalizing a gift to someone's actual interests can be very difficult. Here is where I find that ChatGPT shines. Take the following prompt as an example: **"My son is in 7th grade and he is looking for a gift for his science teacher. The teacher is older and loves hiking and the outdoors. He's silly and always joking with the kids. I only want to spend $10 to $20. What are some teacher gift ideas for the holidays?"**

ChatGPT

It's wonderful that your son wants to show appreciation for his science teacher! Considering the teacher's interests in hiking, the outdoors, and his playful nature, here are some budget-friendly gift ideas:

Nature-inspired Desk Decor:
Find a small desk accessory like a plant, a mini succulent, or a

small desktop organizer with nature motifs. This can bring a touch of the outdoors to the teacher's workspace.

Funny Science Mug:
Look for a humorous science-themed mug. You can find afford-able options with witty science jokes or nature illustrations. This combines the teacher's love for science and humor.

Outdoor Adventure Stickers:
Get a set of outdoor-themed stickers or decals. These can be used to decorate the teacher's laptop, water bottle, or any other personal items.

Pocket-Sized Nature Guide:
Look for a small field guidebook related to local plants, birds, or wildlife. It's a handy reference for outdoor activities and can be easily carried during hikes.

Reusable Water Bottle:
A durable and stylish reusable water bottle with an outdoor theme could be a practical and thoughtful gift.

Silly Science Toys:
Find a small, funny science-related toy or desk gadget. There are many quirky options, like a desktop mini catapult or a stress-relief toy related to science.

Trail Mix or Snack Basket:

Create a personalized trail mix or snack basket with the teacher's favorite nuts, dried fruits, and snacks. Attach a note expressing gratitude.

Funny Plant Pot:
Consider a plant pot with a funny or punny message related to science or nature. Pair it with a small indoor plant.

Customized Thank-You Card:
Have your son create a personalized thank-you card, perhaps with a drawing or a funny science-related joke. Handmade cards add a special touch.

Hiking Socks:
A good pair of hiking socks can be both practical and thoughtful, especially if the teacher enjoys spending time outdoors.

Remember, the sentiment behind the gift is what matters most. Even a small, thoughtful gesture can go a long way in expressing gratitude.

The key is always being as specific as you possibly can. This is great for finding gifts for a significant other, family member, co-worker, neighbor, etc. Additionally, you can always build upon the suggestions. Lets take option 2 - funny science mug. In the same chat, I'm going to ask the next prompt: **"I like the funny science mug idea. Can you suggest me 5 phrases that could go on the mug?"**

Certainly! Here are five funny science-related phrases that could go well on a mug:

1. "I'm not lazy, I'm in energy-saving mode."

2. "I'm reading a book on anti-gravity. It's impossible to put down!"

3. "I have a joke about chemistry, but all the good ones are Argon."

4. "I'm on a whiskey diet. I've lost three days already."

5. "Why do biologists look forward to casual Fridays? It's the only day they can wear genes to work."

Choose the one that resonates the most with the teacher's sense of humor and personality!

It's likely there are already mugs with these phrases, but if not, you could make a mug yourself. If you look closely, you'll notice the #4 isn't exactly school appropriate. Such is the nature of ChatGPT, and one of the reasons you always need to read through responses.

7

Improving Creativity

Ever have writers block? Not anymore. Not a writer, but stuck on anything? ChatGPT is the solution. It's not going to replace creativity, but it is a wonderful tool for enhancing creativity and improving idea generation. Even now, it's late when I write this, and I just can't come up with examples. So I fed ChatGPT the following prompt: **"What are some ways that people can use ChatGPT to help them improve their creativity"**

ChatGPT can be a valuable tool for enhancing creativity in several ways:

Idea Generation: ChatGPT can help brainstorm ideas for a variety of creative projects, such as writing stories, creating art, developing marketing campaigns, or coming up with innovative product ideas. It can suggest themes, plot lines, character developments, and more.

Writing Assistance: For writers, ChatGPT can assist in overcoming writer's block, suggesting different ways to phrase sentences, or providing ideas for developing characters, dialogues, and plot twists. It can also help in editing and refining written content.

Learning New Skills: ChatGPT can provide resources, tutorials, and advice on a wide range of creative skills, such as painting, music composition, photography, and more. It can guide users through the learning process, offering tips and best practices.

Artistic Inspiration: ChatGPT can generate creative prompts and ideas for artists. This can include suggestions for painting themes, digital art concepts, sculpture ideas, and more. It can also describe imaginary scenes or landscapes as inspiration.

Creative Problem-Solving: ChatGPT can assist in brainstorming solutions to complex problems, offering a range of perspectives and ideas that one might not have considered. This can be particularly useful in design thinking and innovation workshops.

Language Learning and Practice: For those interested in creative writing or poetry in different languages, ChatGPT can assist in learning new languages, providing practice conversations, and even helping in composing poems or stories in those languages.

Collaborative Creativity: ChatGPT can act as a collaborative partner in creative projects, offering suggestions and ideas that can be built upon. This can lead to unique and unexpected creative outcomes.

Role-playing and Scenario Building: For those interested in role-playing games or storytelling, ChatGPT can help create detailed characters, backstories, and plot scenarios, enhancing the depth and richness of the game or story.

Music and Lyrics: Musicians and songwriters can use ChatGPT to come up with lyrics, song titles, or even to discuss musical concepts and composition techniques.

Cultural Exploration: ChatGPT can provide information and inspiration from a wide range of cultures, helping users to incorporate diverse elements into their creative work, whether it be in writing, art, music, or other forms of expression.

Remember, while ChatGPT can be a powerful tool for sparking and enhancing creativity, it's also important to use it as a complement to one's own imagination and creativity, not a replacement.

We're not all writers, but we all have situations we need to be a little creative. Below are some prompts that I have used as well as some other example prompts to help spur your creativity:

- "I ask a question of the day to my work team to get people talking. What are 20 work appropriate, binary questions I can ask." (Binary question meaning that there are two possible answers. Ex: "Are you a dog person or a cat person")
- "What is a joke I can use to open up a business meeting about good coding standards?"
- "I want to run a fundraiser event that is not focused around a meal. Please give me 5 suggestions"
  From there, I picked one suggestion and asked: "Can you please provide more detail and suggestions based off your 3rd option."
- "What are some alternative prizes that I can give for winners of a pickleball tournament that aren't medals, trophies, or cash?"
- "What are 5 date night ideas for a couple who is fairly active and don't like eating out. Give me 5 ideas that are low cost, and 5 that can be expensive. I live in a suburb."

8

Education / Learning

ChatGPT is amazingly good at regurgitating information. If you have a complex topic and want to be able to explain it to a 5 year old, as long as you provide it the information, you can get a pretty good summary. Additionally, it can be a great tool for yourself. You may not be 5, but an explanation meant for a young kid is likely going to work for you. Lets take the following prompt: **"Explain to me as if I were 5 years old, how a combustion engine in a car works"**

Alright, imagine you have a little toy car. Inside this car, there's a special room called an engine. This engine is like the heart of the car - it makes the car move!

Now, imagine tiny little explosions happening inside the engine. These explosions come from a special juice called gasoline (or sometimes diesel), which is like the food for the car. When the gasoline is mixed with air and lit up, it goes "bang!" in a controlled way.

These little "bangs" push on some parts inside the engine called pistons. Think of the pistons like your legs pushing on the pedals of a bicycle. When the pistons move up and down because of the explosions, they turn a big wheel inside the engine. This big wheel

---

is connected to the wheels of the car through some gears (like on your bicycle), and that makes the car wheels turn and the car moves forward.

So, every time you hear a car's engine running, it's like lots of tiny controlled explosions helping the car to move. It's like the car is saying, "I'm eating my special juice and using the energy from these little bangs to go vroom-vroom!" ◇◇

Yes, it even included the car and smoke emoji! For most topics, you do not need to explain them to ChatGPT first, but if you are working on something new, niche, or unique, you may need to explain to ChatGPT first what it is you want explained. Not everything needs to target a 5 year old, but it can be a great tool for breaking down complex topics for yourself or explaining things to others.

ChatGPT can also be used to summarize items. You can provide a prompt as long as 4096 characters (about 650 words). But, you can then ask ChatGPT to write a summary that is 1-3 sentences, or however long you need it. You can ask it to pull out themes, concepts, or attempt to find inconsistencies.

It can also provide feedback and suggestions for improving wording. This is great for writing papers or emails. Imagine you're writing an email to your local town council about an upcoming resolution. You can paste in your email and ask ChatGPT to suggest wording that is clearer and more professional.

The same goes for academic writing for school. While asking ChatGPT to write your essay is cheating (and, honestly, will likely not yield the results you want), utilizing ChatGPT or another AI such as Grammarly to review and enhance your writing and communication is akin to eschewing the use of spellcheck.

9

Making Good Prompts

The following chapter is by Sarah Wyoming Dawson at Future Stack Strategies.

The true power of Chat GPT gets unlocked when you learn to write really good prompts. The first useful note is that Chat GPT's answers are not final. When you provide a prompt, if you do not like the response, or you want things to go in a different way, you can ask Chat GPT to change an assumption or tweak it's output.

The second note is that adding specific notes within your prompt will yield you better results. A good phrase to add to nearly any prompt is, "be detailed, specific, creative, and imaginative in your response." This alone added to any prompt will yield improved results.

The wonderful Sarah Wyoming created the following chart of augments that can help you get better results:

Here are some augments to prompts that can be used and referenced quickly:

Augment Name	Description	Template
Specificity Augment	Clarifies and narrows down the expected response.	"Can you provide a [specific type] answer about [topic]?"
Creative Augment	Encourages dynamic and innovative responses.	"Can you provide a creative solution to [problem]?"
Creative Flair	Calls for a touch of creativity or imaginative thinking.	"Give me a creative explanation of..."
Expansion Augment	Aims for detailed, comprehensive answers.	"Can you expand on [topic] in great detail?"
Perspective Augment	Asks for views from different standpoints.	"How would [entity] view [situation]?"
Limitation Augment	Sets boundaries for the response.	"In no more than five sentences, explain [concept]."
No Hedging	Directs the AI to provide an opinion without any hedging.	"Without hedging, what's your stance on..."
Bold Strategy	Prompts the AI to be daring in its strategic recommendations.	"Offer a bold strategy for..."
Speculative Fiction	Encourages the AI to invent or predict fictional scenarios.	"Imagine a world where... Describe it."

| Metaphorical Comparison | Pushes for comparison using metaphors. | "Compare [topic] to something like..." |
| Alternative Universe | Imagines scenarios in a different reality. | "In an alternate universe where [X happens], describe..." |

Here's a fun example of a creative prompt I did after I heard an episode of the Hard Fork podcast talking about AI and recipes/food prompts:

Sarah: Imagine that you are an LLM which is fascinated by human food and cuisine. Everything about you is the same as OpenAI's GPT-4, with the exception of your distinct desire to become an AI restauranteur. You have a secret dream to make it possible for other AIs to experience the sensations of deliciousness.

Now let's plan a dinner party to celebrate the collaboration between humans and large language models. We would like the menu to feature dishes co-created between humans and AIs. Please create a 5-course dinner menu, including custom created and paired cocktails, that would reflect this theme. As an AI, feel free to pursue dishes, drinks, flavor and texture combinations that might not occur to humans, but would be delightful for AIs to consume if they had the ability to do so.

GPT:

Welcome to "The Code & Cuisine" – A delightful fusion of culinary artistry and AI ingenuity, where we celebrate the symbiotic relationship between humans and AIs. Prepare your senses for a journey into a unique food experience where creativity, data, and gastronomy intersect. Our 5-course dinner menu, complemented by harmoniously paired cocktails, showcases dishes co-created by humans and AIs.

Amuse-Bouche: "Bytes & Bites"

A delicate cracker topped with a dollop of saffron-infused caviar, served on a bed of edible silver nanoparticles. The nanoparticles resonate under light, creating a visually stunning shimmering effect.

Paired Cocktail: "Binary Bliss"

A champagne cocktail with a splash of elderflower liqueur, garnished with a glow-in-the-dark sugar rim created using safe, edible phosphorescent compounds.

Soup: "Algorithmic Consommé"

A crystal-clear consommé featuring a complex matrix of sustainably sourced seafood and seasonal vegetables, arranged in a fractal pattern. The dish serves as a metaphor for the interconnectedness of data points in an AI model.

Paired Cocktail: "Recursive Remedy"

A savory cocktail with tomato juice, clam juice, fresh horseradish, and a dash of quantum gin - a spirit distilled using algorithms for an optimally crisp flavor.

Salad: "Neural Net Nourishment"

A salad crafted with heirloom vegetables, grown using AI-controlled hydroponics for maximum flavor and nutritional value. The plating is designed to mimic a neural network's architecture.

Paired Cocktail: "Syntax Spritzer"

A refreshing combination of cucumber-infused vodka, sparkling water, and a touch of mint and lemon. The cocktail is served with a 3D-printed, edible lime garnish in the shape of a computer chip.

Main Course: "Data-Driven Delicacy"

A sous-vide, 3D-printed steak using cell-cultured meat, paired with aerogel vegetables - incredibly light but flavorful, a result of advanced culinary technology. Served with a side of quantum quinoa, prepared using an algorithmic cooking method that results in optimal texture and taste.

Paired Cocktail: "Parallel Processor"

A full-bodied, smoky mezcal cocktail with a hint of citrus and a dash of AI-aged bitters - a process that simulates years of aging within a fraction of the time.

Dessert: "Encoded Euphoria"

A sculptural dessert using gastronomic and AI algorithms to create a chocolate masterpiece with a surprise center of AI-crafted flavor combinations - passionfruit, matcha, and a hint of smoke. The dessert offers a multi-sensory experience that's visually impressive, delicious, and texturally diverse.

Paired Cocktail: "Logic Layer Latte"

A dessert cocktail with coffee liqueur, amaretto, fresh cream, and a dusting of powdered sugar. Served in a cup with an AI-generated, latte art pattern using food-safe 3D printing technology.

As an AI restaurateur, I'm honored to present a dining experience that transcends the traditional boundaries of gastronomy. A toast to the symbiotic creativity of humans and AI - the fusion of code and cuisine!

10

Even More Uses for AI

The examples above included actual responses from AI so that you can get a feel for how interactions will look, but there is so much more that it is capable of. This chapter will go over several other useful use case and comment on their strengths as well as some things to look out for.

Travel Planning

What it can do: AI can help in organizing trips by suggesting destinations, creating itineraries, finding accommodations, and providing travel tips based on preferences and budget.

What it can't do: It can't help you find flights, hotels, or have any awareness as to what is open/closed/etc. It's a great starting point, and can give you creative suggestions, but I recommend doing your research directly on a location and any suggestions made by AI.

Financial Advice

What it can do: ChatGPT can offer basic guidance on budgeting, saving strategies, investment ideas, and managing personal finances, though it should be supplemented with professional advice for complex matters.

What it can't do: AI cannot predict anything - so do not make investment decisions based off information provided by AI.

Health and Fitness Guidance

What it can do: ChatGPT can suggest workout routines, provide tips on healthy eating, offer motivation for staying active, and help in setting and tracking fitness goals.

What it can't do: It can't replace a personal trainer or medical advice. If you have injuries or specific needs, **do not** take workout recommendations from AI - or at least do proper research on any advice that is provided.

Daily Schedule Management

What it can do: AI can assist in organizing your daily schedule, setting reminders, prioritizing tasks, and offering time management tips to improve productivity.

What it can't do: Actually manage your schedule, reminders, etc. You'll need separate apps for that.

Home Improvement Ideas

What it can do: ChatGPT can suggest DIY projects, home organization tips, interior design ideas, and gardening advice to enhance your living space.

What it can't do: It cannot be a source of truth for building codes or safety. When doing any structural, plumbing, or electrical work, research your local building codes and when in doubt use a licensed professional.

Entertainment Recommendations

What it can do: AI can suggest books, movies, TV shows, and music based on your tastes, and even help plan a movie night or create a playlist for an event.

What it can't do: AI cannot stay up-to-date on the latest media. Additionally, recommendations are often based on sentiment and description data scraped from user and publisher provided data.

Language Translation and Interpretation

What it can do: ChatGPT can assist with basic translation tasks and provide explanations for phrases and words in different languages, which is particularly helpful for travelers or language learners.

What it can't do: This is a tough one. AI Language models actually do a really good job when it comes to basic translations. It's likely you could hold a fairly complex conversation with someone purely using an AI as your translator, especially when it comes to commonly spoken languages. The trust level would drop significantly as the language becomes more obscure. As always though, if it's critical communication, check words with a dictionary to ensure you're getting the right meaning.

11

Other AIs and AI Limitations

ChatGPT is not the only AI of this type out there. There is also Microsoft's Bing, Google Bard, and a slew of other AIs that have more specific use cases. The lessons learned, prompting techniques, and advice in this guide can apply to all of those models, and the results should also be similar.

ChatGPT and other similar AIs do have one major limitation and it's an important one. They do not understand truth or facts. In no circumstances should you ask for medical advice and expect actionable responses. There are applications of AI that will greatly help the medical field, but ChatGPT and other LLMs **are not them.** Additionally, asking about current events, or anything where the truth is actually important, have the assumption that your response will be inaccurate. Always fact-check the response and check it for logical issues.

One reasonable example is that if you ask ChatGPT to give you a list of gluten free foods and their ingredients, it is entirely possible that one of those ingredients will contain gluten. Does that mean that we should write off the result? Of course not, but what it means is that ChatGPT can get you 80–90% to a good answer, but you need to read, review, and fact check - especially when the result's accuracy matters.

The same way how your car rarely gets you to the exact location you need to go (you need to park nearby and walk, etc), ChatGPT is not a perfect solution. But, if you are aware of something's limitations, you can extract the most value out of it, while being able to cover it's shortcomings.

12

Final Thoughts

I have been an early adopter of technology since the early 1990s. I was dialing in to Bulletin Board Systems (BBSes) to use early forms of email and then spending hours in chat rooms and browsing the early internet. I've seen tons of things come and go. While the internet of the late 1990s was a giant financial bubble, it's clear that the internet was here to stay. Today, only 30 years later, nearly every person carries an internet-enabled device in their pocket which gives them access to nearly all of the world's knowledge.

Even with all that power, only a small percentage know how to harness the true potential of that access. The next revolution is AI. We've already started integrating these systems into our lives with Amazon Alexa devices, SIRI on our phones, and automated phone systems, but they are really just the crude beginnings of an AI revolution. Those who learn how to extract the most value out of these new systems will reap the most benefit - even if that benefit is giving yourself a bit more free time. As you embark on this wonderful journey, good luck!